D0381416

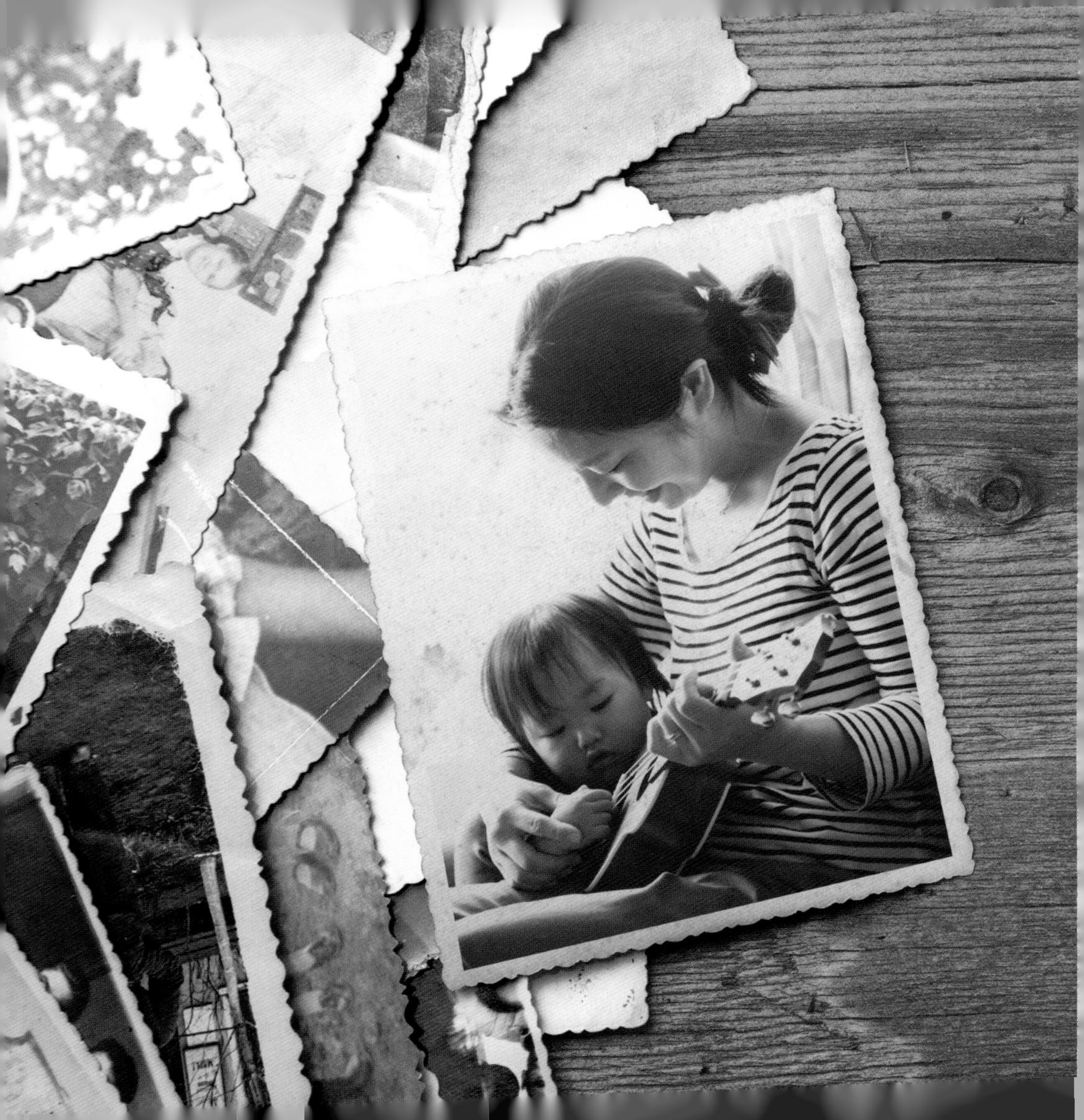

When I sat down to write what would become "She Put the Music in Me," I knew I wanted to write a song not only *about* my mom, but *for* my mom. By the time I sat in the studio, contemplating the direction I wanted the song to go in with my producer and friend, Aaron, my mom had been battling cancer for months. I desperately wanted to feel inspired, but instead I felt exhausted. I was completely *empty*. I wondered how on earth was I going to create the song I wanted to when I felt so *depleted* and *heartbroken* in the wake of her failing health.

When Aaron suggested that Primary songs be the foundation for our creative process, I loved the idea.

"What about this hook: 'she put the music in me'?" he suggested.

I'm so thankful that God was able to pour that specific inspiration into Aaron in that moment. I've often wondered if my grief was *too thick* for my own heart to hear it.

What followed was a *beautiful* walk through memories of songs that I'd been taught since childhood. The stories and pictures that came to my mind as I scanned through Primary songs and chose each line was like watching a movie reel of my life. And once I began writing, the process flowed easily—as if the song was willing itself into existence. It felt like a *gift*.

My mom passed away just a few short weeks after the song was recorded.

*Heavenly Father
sent her to me*

*And she taught me to
lift up my
voice and sing*

I never dreamed that "She Put the Music in Me" would touch the number of lives that it has. It was just a song that I wrote for Mom, to say *thank you.* It has meant the world to me to know that others are gifting this song to their own mothers as a way to say the same.

So, to all mothers of every kind: Thank you for putting the music in the hearts of those you love.

She gives me the hope of a life yet to be

SHE PUT THE *music* IN ME

REFLECTIONS ON MOTHERHOOD

I remember getting ready to leave the hospital after giving birth to my firstborn and tearfully confessing to my nurses that "We have *no idea* what we're doing!" as they escorted us out of the hospital. I'm sure my confession came as a result of a combination of fatigue and postpartum hormones, but I figured that if I came clean about being clueless, they might let me stay for a few more days and figure it out in the presence of trained professionals.

Do you know what those nurses did? They didn't gasp in shock and horror as I thought they might. They didn't even flinch. They just laughed, gave me a hug, and *assured me* that I'd be fine as they checked that I'd installed the car seat correctly and waved goodbye.

All my studying and research and preparation during pregnancy felt completely *inadequate* when brought face to face with the tiny living, breathing life that I was now responsible for. I wished over and over again—just like many new mothers do—that my baby had come with a manual in those first few years. The biggest lesson that early motherhood taught me, however, was that raising a baby doesn't require mandatory professional expertise or exhaustive research.

Being a successful mother comes with only one, universal requirement: *to love first.* If you love first, everything else follows naturally.

*It started with
rock-a-bye,
comforting when
I'd cry*

All in her own style

As time went on and my challenges morphed from newborn exhaustion to anxieties over early childhood development and beyond, my relationship with God became the parenting manual I had wished for when she was first born. I realized that even the most "perfect" mothers are just figuring it out as they go and that the healthiest, best-adjusted kids I knew came from homes that looked and functioned differently—but whose *foundation was love:* for God, and for each other. The mothers I admired and looked up to the most were women who trusted their gut and listened for the whisperings of the *Spirit* to guide them in raising their kids. These women trusted the divine gifts of motherhood given to them by an all-knowing and all-loving Creator. And they trusted Him to lead them through their daily motherhood *journey.*

And she built my house on a rock

And she lives all that she taught

And she is all that a woman should be

And she lives to search, ponder, pray

And she gives every day

Motherhood has required me to *be more* than I was before having children—more patient, more loving, more compassionate, more energetic, more flexible, more gracious (both in extending grace to my children and in giving it to myself in all of my failings). The way motherhood has stretched and depleted and pulled me has felt endless at times. I've read self-help books and blogs, I've read studies and confided in close friends, I've taken time for myself and invested in my mental health . . . and yet the most helpful and meaningful investment I've made in my own motherhood has come as I've *relied on my Savior* to refill my empty cup over and over again.

ALL KINDS
OF MOTHERS

Very little of my own motherhood experience has been what I *dreamed* it would be as a little girl: the timing of my motherhood, a baby born with chronic health issues, high-risk pregnancies, spending a season as a single mother, and becoming a stepmom to four beautiful kids who lost their own mother to an early and unexpected death have all been part of *my experience* as a mother.

I was sitting in church one Sunday when one of my twin boys—he was five at the time—snuggled up under my arm and looked up at me with big blue eyes. He asked, *"Do you know where my mommy is?"*

My mama heart wrenched in my chest as I looked down at him and answered. "Yeah, buddy, . . . she's in heaven. Do you know who else is there?" I asked him.

He waited.

"*My* mom."

I don't pretend to understand why God would take the mother of four young beautiful children to heaven so early, just like I can't fathom why He would need to take my mom the way that He did—but in that moment, I felt the beauty and sacredness of being able to *connect* with another precious child of God through a shared heartbreak and experience.

I knew He was really there

He heard my child's prayer

Answering from up above

I have learned for myself as a stepmom that God uses us as women to mother *throughout our lives*—sometimes through the children we birth and raise. Sometimes through other women's children we raise. Sometimes through other women's children that we *love.*

She gave like a little stream

I was her sunbeam

And I felt my Savior's love

I had zero expectation that my father would remarry after my mother's death. When my father announced his engagement, I braced myself for the challenge of *opening my heart* and family to a new member. I won't pretend that I was particularly gracious or happy during that season of my life. I was grieving, and grief is often messy and ugly. My stepmother *was* gracious, though, thankfully, and that graciousness paved the way for our eventual friendship. It's been several years since my father remarried and almost a decade since my mother passed away, and I can say truthfully that I can't imagine my family without my stepmother. I love and appreciate all the ways she has *mothered* me since becoming a part of it.

I saw her kneel and pray with our family every day

Listening to each whispered word

"While *we* tend to equate motherhood solely with maternity, in the Lord's language, the word *mother* has layers of meaning. Of all the words they could have chosen to define her role and her essence, both God the Father and Adam called Eve 'the mother of all living'—and they did so *before* she ever bore a child. Like Eve, our motherhood began before we were born. . . . Motherhood is more than bearing children, though it is certainly that. It is the essence of who we are as women. It defines our very identity, our divine stature and nature, and the unique traits our Father gave us. . . . If we really want to make a *difference* [in the world], it will happen as we mother those we have borne and those we are willing to bear with." —Sheri Dew

Leading me, guiding me,
walking beside me, she helped me
To walk in the light

I am awestruck that a loving God invites us to be cocreators with Him. And we, as women, can exercise our divine motherhood in a multitude of ways in this life. The Lord's grace is *sufficient* for all our heartbreaks, our shortcomings, our disappointments, and our failures in motherhood. I believe with all my heart that if we love God and His children with all of our hearts first, that every other part of our divine development will *fall into place.*

We *will* become who He has planned for us to become in this lifetime . . . and I believe there is so much more in the life to come—with all the mothers who came before us.

SHE PUT THE
MUSIC IN ME

It started with rock-a-bye,

comforting when I'd cry

All in her own style

Then popcorn before my eyes,

turning frowns upside down

Into smiles

With songs of the birds up high,

looking at the blue, blue sky

The wind as it rushes by

Then leading me,
guiding me,
walking beside me,
she helped me

To walk in the light

And she built my house on a rock

And she lives all that she taught

And she is all that a woman should be

SHE PUT THE *music* IN ME

I knew He was really there

He heard my child's prayer

Answering from up above

She gave like a little stream

I was her sunbeam

And I felt my Savior's love

I saw her kneel and pray with our
family every day
Listening to each whispered word

Gentle in deed and thought,
all the things Jesus taught
Following promptings she heard

And she lives to search, ponder, pray

And she gives every day

So her thanks will always

be thanks indeed

SHE PUT THE *music* IN ME

He made the tiny wings of each
little bird that sings
In the leafy treetops up high

And all creatures great and small,
I know God made them all

Because of her sweet lullabies

She's like a star shining bright

And helps me to choose the right

And she gives me the hope of a life yet to be

SHE PUT THE *music* IN ME

She is so good to me

        Heavenly Father sent her to me

And she taught me to lift up

        my voice and sing

SHE PUT THE *music* IN ME

IMAGE CREDITS

pp. 4–5, 14–15, 16, 27–28, 32–33, 37, 38, 40–41, 45: OKing/Shutterstock.com

p. 5: AleksandarNakic/Getty Images

p. 6: kohei_hara/Getty Images

pp. 6, 12–13: ADragan/Shutterstock.com

pp. 8, 20: photka/Shutterstock.com

p. 9: Tetra Images - Mike Kemp/ Getty Images

p. 10: Mike Kurtz/Getty Images

p. 10: Andrii Zastrozhnov/Shutterstock.com

p. 11: Shanina/Getty Images

p. 11: Courtesy of the Robert R. Gibby family, used with permission

p. 12: Cavan Images/Getty Images

p. 15: Siri Stafford/Getty Images

p. 17: Tetra Images/Getty Images

p. 17: ArjaKo's/Shutterstock.com

p. 18: RyanJLane/Getty Images

p. 18: Martin Novak/Shutterstock.com

pp. 18, 24: inxti/Shutterstock.com

pp. 20, 30: Lora liu/Shutterstock.com

p. 21: Courtesy of Madi McCann, photo by Ashley Bridgewater, used with permission

p. 22: aunaauna/Getty Images

p. 23: brickrena/Shutterstock.com

p. 25: Courtesy of the Dorothy E. Gibby family, used with permission

p. 25: Roger Johnson/Getty Images

p. 25: Ramiro Olaciregui/Getty Images

p. 25: Tuan Tran/Getty Images

p. 27: Pazargic Liviu/Shutterstock.com

p. 28: d3sign/Getty Images

p. 28: Merydolla/Shutterstock.com

p. 30: Vera Petrunina/Shutterstock.com

p. 31: Hary/Shutterstock.com

p. 32: DNY59/Getty Images

p. 33: Jill Lehmann Photography/ Getty Images

p. 33: ESB Professional/Shutterstock.com

p. 34: Andrey Yurlov/Shutterstock.com

p. 35: Courtesy of Jennifer Campbell, photo by Kelsi Greef, used with permission

p. 35: A3pfamily/Shutterstock.com

p. 36: Courtesy of Ashley Gould, photo by Megan Harrison, used with permission

p. 36: Courtesy of Lauren Eyre, photo by Marie Long, used with permission

p. 36: Courtesy of Sarah Otuonye, used with permission

pp. 36, 42–43, 48: P Maxwell Photography/Shutterstock.com

p. 36: Marek Tr/Shutterstock.com

p. 38, 45: Odua Images/Shutterstock.com

p. 39: d3sign/Getty Images

p. 39: sociologas/Shutterstock.com

p. 40: martinedoucet/Getty Images

p. 40: A3pfamily/Shutterstock.com

p. 41: Klaus Vedfelt/Getty Images

p. 41: Jose Luis Pelaez Inc/Getty Images

p. 42: JGI/Jamie Grill/Getty Images

p. 42: Courtesy of Emily Remington, used with permission

p. 42: rangizzz/Shutterstock.com

p. 43: gradyreese/Getty Images

p. 44: Tolga TEZCAN/Getty Images

p. 44: GCShutter/Getty Images

p. 48: Courtesy of Calee Reed, used with permission

SOURCES

p. 29, *the mother of all living:* Moses 4:26.

p. 29, *While we tend to equate motherhood:* Sheri L. Dew, "Are We Not All Mothers?" *Ensign*, November 2011.

CALEE REED ADAMS

grew up in San Diego, California, and was taught to sing by her mother at a very young age. When Calee's mother passed away in 2011 after a battle with cancer, Calee decided to write her first album, *The Waiting Place,* as a tribute to her. Since then, she has released several additional albums, including *What Heaven Feels Like, Believer,* and *Rejoice!* (a Christmas album). After experiencing the pain of a divorce and the challenges of life as a single mom, Calee married Jon Adams, a widower with four children, in 2017. She continues to write and perform inspirational music in between the joys (and chaos!) of blending a family with six adorable children.